111 Ways to Save

"I took your advice about how to save even more at Kohl's. I found the section with the 70-80% off women's clothing and it didn't take long to look through the racks for some dresses, tops and sweaters that I needed. I tried everything on, made my selections, and headed to the register with my 30% off coupon from being a Kohl's charge customer.

I bought 6 items including a dress and purse, saved $331 off the original total, plus an extra $32 with the 30% off coupon. I'm very excited to update my wardrobe without breaking our budget!! Thanks so much for your great suggestion."

Vicki, Texas

"Earlier this year I realized that I had forgotten all about the frequent flier miles I still had with American Airlines. That probably happened because I have lived abroad for several years and had been collecting points with another airline. Then, a friend of mine suggested we go to Berlin for a long weekend over Easter and he had expiring points to use for our flights. His suggestion along with me reading Jill's newsletter to remind me that I too, had points to use. So we got 4 nights in a Berlin hotel with my miles. Since I still had miles left, I used those for another short trip to Mallorca with another friend. I got my flight and then used the last of the miles to rent us a car for 2 days, so we could explore the island outside of the main city of Palma. So, don't forget to use those points and miles you have accumulated. And if done well enough in advance, you can book decent hotels and flights at reasonable times of the day."

Heidi, Denmark

"The tips of the week by Jill Foster are great. I never realized that gift cards are interchangeable between sister stores. Now I can buy what I really want. This is a must read."

Denise, Connecticut

"Having followed Jill's blog and website, she has helped us save money, doing very simple things such as only having cash when going shopping or eating out, as Jill says you cannot spend more then you have with you, so you can budget better. Also making sure phone chargers and TV plugs are unplugged when not at home, it all adds up to more savings each month, that would have been left on."

"Jill Foster is incredibly good at teaching ways to save money and to manage the money you have. Her amazing on-line tips have helped me be more mindful about how I spend and manage my money. Her practical suggestions have helped me with budget tracking, impulse buying, keeping track of my monthly bills, and with being more conscious of options for saving money. And a number of my teen clients have learned valuable lessons about money from her book, Cash, Credit and Your Finances: The Teen Years."

111

WAYS TO SAVE

Jill Russo Foster

111 Ways to Save

Money Pit, LLC
2016

First Edition

DISCLAIMER

This book details the author's personal experiences with and opinions about economical living. The author is not a licensed financial consultant.

The author and publisher are providing this book and its contents on an "as is" basis and make no representations or warranties of any kind with respect to this book or its contents. The author and publisher disclaim all such representations and warranties, including for example warranties of merchantability and financial advice for a particular purpose. In addition, the author and publisher do not represent or warrant that the information accessible via this book is accurate, complete or current.

The statements made about products and services have not been evaluated by the U.S. government. Please consult with your own Certified Public Accountant, Attorney, or Financial Advisor regarding the suggestions and recommendations made in this book.

Except as specifically stated in this book, neither the author or publisher, nor any authors, contributors, or other representatives will be liable for

111 Ways to Save

My thanks to the many clients, colleagues and friends, who have stood by me with unwavering support and encouragement to write this book. To all who gave me suggestions and tips, thank you.

Thank you to all

Table of Contents

FOREWARD

My hope is that you read this book and follow the tips that appeal to you. You don't need to do each and every tip. Work on what's important to you at this point in your life. This book is not meant to be a burden. It's to improve your finances. Everyone starts from where they are. There is no shame, guilt or blame for what has happened to you in the past.

Today is the start of the next phase of your financial life. Starting today, you will make informed choices that are right for you. Just paying attention to your finances and making conscious choices will improve your financial picture. Good money habits begin with new information that leads to better choices.

Ask yourself, "What is the one thing I need to do now to improve my finances?" Take a moment to come up with the answer. That is what you should focus on first. Good luck on your journey to improve your financial situation.

INTRODUCTION - MY STORY

I was born and raised in Fairfield County, Connecticut. My father was a hard working man who worked two jobs, as far back as I can remember. My mother was a bookkeeper and handled all the family finances. We were a very close family who lived a modest lifestyle with occasional splurges on education, food, clothing and vacations.

When I should have been learning about money in my teens, my mother was diagnosed with a terminal illness. My first job after college, I went right from college to banking, starting as a teller. I began my career in a very affluent area with clients that were celebrities, professional athletes etc. I watched how they lived. They drove the cars I wanted and wore the most beautiful designer clothes, but they were also on the overdraft list every day. You can imagine me being tempted by all of this because I had no financial guidance.

When my mother passed away, I inherited some money which I foolishly wasted on living the life-style. I thought I wanted. And when that money ran out, I got credit cards and continued that same lifestyle, until I maxed out 27 credit cards.

I was in trouble. Life, as I knew it, had to change. But how was I going to pay off 27 maxed out credit cards? I was in my 20's, so you know I didn't want to be home every night or not wear the latest fashion. I was in the financial field, so bankruptcy wasn't an option. I would lose my job and career if my credit suffered.

So I had to make some radical changes. I got a part time job and an occasional third job to be able to pay more than the minimum on this debt.

Eventually years later, I got it all paid off.

Then I chose to work for myself. With self employment came many more financial challenges. My first business was a standard client services model, which made it difficult to create a financial plan because my income was so unreliable. How do you budget when there is no money coming in this month or when clients are not paying you on a timely basis? I chose to close that business and started my mortgage company, The Mortgage Arrangers, LLC where money collection was not going to be an issue. I still had the peaks and valleys of cash flow depending on how the home buying market was going. Some months I had extra money while others were a bit short, which was a challenge, but at least when a mortgage closed I knew I was going to get paid.

I needed a plan to live by and I had to figure out what was important to me. I needed to learn how I could have what I wanted and still have fun while living within my means. So that became my mission. I have made many mistakes, but fortunately I have learned from all of them. To this day, my husband and I still do many things that are low cost like going to movies in the park, using the services of the public library and having pot luck dinners with friends. We choose to live frugally, but we do have planned splurges so that we don't feel deprived.

As you can see, just like most people, I have had (and continue to have) issues with debt, not saving as much as I want, keeping my emergency savings built up and dealing with things I want but probably don't really need. My goal for this book is to share with you what I have learned and how I deal with the everyday problems of managing my finances.

I personally use many of the tips in this book. My January ritual is to see where my husband and I are at financially and to reassess our bills. I am always looking for more ways to save money. My credit report has always been (and will continue to be) important to me. Just like you, I am tempted by sales and discounted items. I have to take time to decide if something is really a bargain and if I really need it. Just because something is a great buy, doesn't mean I should buy it. I have to continuously remind myself of this.

As you work through this book, please contact me with your thoughts and questions.

Please send your comments to:

Book@JillRussoFoster.com.

I look forward to hearing from you.

Jill Russo Foster, Money Pit, LLC

www.JillRussoFoster.com

Home

1. Make your own cleaning supplies. You can save big with ingredients as simple as distilled vinegar, baking soda and/or lemon (which you probably already have in your home). For example, distilled vinegar mixed with water is a great glass cleaner and distilled vinegar with baking soda is great for carpet stains. There are many cost effective solutions for making your own cleaning supplies. Check them out online.

2. Ask if there is a discount for paying in cash. Our heating oil company gives us 10¢ off per gallon if we pay in cash the day the oil is delivered. Heating bills can add up and so can the savings. Many gas stations charge one price for cash and a higher one for credit. It never hurts to ask, the worst they can say is no.

3. Are you planning a home improvement project or replacing an appliance? You might be eligible for a rebate and/or a tax credit. Search the internet to see if there's something available for you. You can also check with your utility company or state energy department about rebates, tax credits and/or special financial

options available. These special deals change every year, so watch the dates, and make sure you check a few months into the year and again later, as things are always changing.

4. Think your interest rate is too high on your mortgage? Call your mortgage company and make your case: "I have been a good customer for XX years and have always paid on time. Is there a way to get my interest rate lowered by modifying our mortgage?" The person you are speaking with may not have the authority to help you, so you may have to ask for a supervisor. Be polite and don't threaten to take your business elsewhere unless you are actually prepared to follow through. If it doesn't work, you can always call again and speak with someone else for another try. You will never know unless you try and this may lower your interest rate.

5. Think home maintenance. Spend some time each and every month doing upkeep which will save you from major repairs. Regular upkeep will save you both time and money. For example, check and replace the grout and caulk in your bathrooms before you have a leak that may require a whole new tile wall. Clean behind and

under your appliances – we regularly vacuum under the fridge and the dryer vent to remove the dust build-up, which can cause problems with your appliances.

6. Learn to do small repairs around the house. If you have a big project, check at your local major home improvement store to see if they offer classes. If you want to tackle a project without taking a class, the employees at the home improvement stores may have helpful tips and advice. Any maintenance or repair you do yourself will save you money. Remember not to do anything that you are not comfortable with. For example, if you don't like heights, it might be better to hire a painter to do the outside painting of your house.

7. Do you have more home than you need? Consider downsizing your home or renting the extra space for additional income. Remember to do your due diligence if you decide to rent out a room, as you are letting a stranger into your home with all your belongings.

8. Do you pay your own utilities? Most local utility companies will do a no or low cost energy audit

to help you save money. We did it. We paid $75 and they replaced all the light bulbs, caulked all the windows and doors for air leaks and mounted door sweeps to stop the drafts. These small improvements would have cost so much more if we had hired someone to do it. Check with your state energy department for information about this.

9. Unplug your small appliances. We use a power strip on our TVs so we can completely turn them off when we aren't watching - TV's are notorious for drawing standby power which means they use electricity even when they aren't turned on. Most of our small kitchen appliances are only plugged in when we use them. We do this throughout our home each day – plugging in the toaster when needed and then unplugging when done. Taking this extra step has easily saved us $20 each month.

10. You can save electricity by air-drying your dishes in the dishwasher. Stop your dishwasher when it gets to the drying cycle, open the dishwasher and let the dishes air dry. Since most drying cycles last 30 minutes, the savings will add up.

11. Keep your thermostat as low as you comfortably can in the winter and as high as you comfortably can in the summer. It will lower your energy costs. You can wear a sweater to keep warm when you lower the thermostat a degree or two. This year we purchased a microfiber sheet set for those cold winter nights. What a pleasure to get into a warm bed. Never turn your heat off in the winter to save money. If your pipes freeze and burst, it will cost you more in the long run.

12. If you don't need hot water, use the cold water handle by itself. When you turn the hot water handle, or combination of the hot and cold handles, you are drawing water from your hot water tank and emptying it just enough to start a water heating cycle. What is you want warm or tepid water? Trust me, you'll most likely get room temperature water in the first few minutes with the cold handle because the water's been sitting in the pipes. Your energy savings will add up with this little cost-saving habit.

13. When you are doing laundry, make sure you run a full load and use cold water to wash your clothes. Consider air-drying your clothes. I personally love the feel of clothes that have been dried outside in the summer months. If you need to use the dryer, do multiple loads back to back to conserve heat.

14. When charging electronics, remember to unplug the cord from the power source in addition to unplugging the electronic item when it's done charging. Don't charge your phone before going to bed as the charger and phone will be plugged in all night and the charging will be finished well before you get up. Chargers without an electronic item attached will still use electricity. And we all have lots of electronics to charge.

Groceries & Food

15. When you put items in your shopping cart, take note of the price. Just today, the advertised price on the cottage cheese was 2 for $4 and the hummus was 2 for $5, but they both rang up incorrectly at the register. I was given 1 of each item for free, and the total was worth about $4.50. I find this happens a lot when I shop on the first day of the sale. You have to know the price of the items you are purchasing so watch the register as the items are scanned. You won't catch this if you are unloading the cart or packing your bags. Pay attention to the scanning process to save yourself money.

16. Have you ever gone in to the store to purchase a specific item that was on sale, only to find out they are out of that item? Ask for a rain check when sale items are out of stock. That way you can go back and get the discounted price on a future trip to the store (usually within a month). I actually file these rain checks along with my coupons in the box that I carry to the store.

17. When you grocery shop, look for yesterday's items. My store sets aside fruits, vegetables, breads, baked goods and meat - all at a substantial discount. My thinking is that I usually shop once a week. Some of the items in my fridge can be as old as a week. Just this week we saved 50% off a loaf of yesterday's bread. Bread in our house lasts a long time, so one day old isn't a problem and it saves us money.

18. You can also look for discontinued items and dented cans to save money at the grocery store. You have to look at what you are purchasing before you decide to buy it. But if it's something you can and will use, you might want to take a look in this area of your store to see what's there. This is especially great with seasonal items that you might want to buy for next year, ahead of time.

19. Being organized saves you money. Have you ever bought something you thought you needed, but when you got home you found you already had it? This can apply to food, clothes, and incidentals - any item in your home. Keep your closet, drawers, and pantry organized so you can easily see the items you need to use. One way to keep your pantry organized is to label the shelves. You know what shelf you keep the canned tuna on, but does everyone else in your household? Take the time to put labels on the lip

of the shelves and that way everything has a place and you can easily see what you need to purchase. Avoiding double purchases will save you money.

20. Combine the grocery store flyer with your coupons to get more savings. Here is one we do often. When tissues are on sale at 88¢ a box, we combine this with a coupon for 50¢ off the purchase of 3. Three boxes cost $2.64 on sale plus an additional $1.00 off with the coupon (my store doubles coupons under a $1). There is also a website www. CTSmartBuys.com for CT that will tell you what is on sale in the grocery store you shop at and let you know when there is a coupon available for those products. All you have to do is save the inserts from the Sunday paper and save them by date. This website tells you which insert the coupon comes from or has a link to download the coupon.

21. Ever run into the grocery store for one or two things and come out with a full bag? This used to happen to me until I figured out that I needed to go in the store without a shopping cart. That way, you can only buy what you can carry.

22. Do you spend more at the grocery store than you planned or more than your budget allows? Shop with cash and leave the debit card at home. If you only have $75 in cash on you, then that's all you can spend. I have found that I am more selective and bargain savvy when shopping with cash. I get only what's on the list - impulse items don't go into the cart and I don't come home with things I don't need or already have.

23. I use coupons. I actually have 2 systems for my coupons. For grocery shopping, I keep my coupons in a small box and take it to the store with me (the same one I file my rain checks in). I am careful not to buy a product just because I have a coupon. This was a hard lesson to learn. Just because I have a coupon, doesn't mean that I need to make the purchase. There will be another coupon or another sale coming in the near future. If I need the product, and I have a coupon, plus it's on sale, I buy it and save money. For non-grocery stores, I keep the coupons clipped to the fridge with a magnet in expiration date order. If we're going shopping, we check the coupons. The expired ones are easy to spot and toss because they're on top. This system works

as I can easily find the coupons when I need them and can toss the expired coupons.

24. Eat at home. Yes, you have heard this one before, but eating at home really is less expensive than eating out or buying takeout. If you have a busy schedule like most of us do, you might believe there's no time to prepare meals. There are many 30 minute meals that are easy to prepare. A little planning ahead makes all the difference. Make soup on your day off and have it ready to heat up when you work late. We make soup on the weekend while doing household chores like the laundry. Think about your time, and you can find ways to cook your own meals. Look at your schedule and think about when you have time to cook. Cook once, eat twice (or more), because you can repurpose the leftovers for another meal. For example, you can roast a chicken for the first night and then use the leftover chicken to top a salad, make chicken salad sandwiches, stir fry, or make chicken tacos for the second or third meal. If you don't want to eat the same ingredients twice in a row, freeze the leftovers for next week. This works well for times when there is no time to cook, because you can just get something out the freezer. Your

own ready- to-eat meals will be much healthier than prepared food from the store.

25. Make your own "convenience" food. Pre-boxed foods and bottled drinks foods are easier, but they usually cost more. We make our own iced tea for the cost of a few tea bags, sugar and water. It's much more cost effective than buying bottled ice tea. We also take leftovers from a meal and freeze a complete meal for the nights when there is no time to cook. Sometimes, portions of items are too big for our family and we freeze into smaller portion size packages. For example, we buy organic berries and eat some and freeze the rest. This makes a great home-made smoothie or lemonade.

26. Grow your own. Yes, you heard me right. For years, we have had a small garden in the summer months to grow our own herbs and vegetables. My family has had a garden for my whole life. We have tomatoes, many varieties of lettuce, peppers, green beans, squash, spinach, parsley, cilantro, rosemary, basil and strawberries. There is nothing as tasty as food picked fresh from your garden. We keep our garden small so it's easy to manage. Anything you grow yourself, you won't have to buy and it costs pennies for seeds

compared to buying the item at the store. We also make our own seeds and use them year to year.

27. When gardening season is over, freeze your leftovers for use later in the year. We make tomato sauce with our extra tomatoes, freeze the berries, and dry the herbs, all to use later in the year. The more you have in the freezer, the less you buy in the year. You can even stretch the growing season by container gardening in your home. It's easy to grow herbs year round on your window sill.

28. Make a meal plan for the week. For our house, we plan 4-5 meals for the week based on the sale flyer from the grocery store. On the unplanned nights, we repurpose the leftovers into another meal. When we shop, we make sure we have all the ingredients needed for cooking and we eliminate the "what's for dinner" question that makes take-out seem so tempting. For a copy of my meal plan worksheet, see the Examples section at the back.

29. One of our biggest splurges is good, quality food – grass fed meats, organic fruits and vegetables, etc. Even so, we manage to stay within our

budget with some planning. We shop at local farms and farmer's markets where we get to know the farmers and how they grow their food. Good food can be more costly, but I believe that you can be healthier and save later on in life with a healthy lifestyle. To find farmer's markets in your area go to www.LocalHarvest.org. Also, remember you can buy yesterday's food, see tip #17.

Bills & Debt

30. Some services allow you to choose a discounted annual payment over a monthly payment. Think car insurance, real estate taxes, life and long term care insurance, etc. Change to - Paying an entire year in advance may sound difficult, but it's possible. A bill of $1,200 annually is really only $100 a month saved and that is easy to work into your budget. Simply divide the annual bill by 12 and make monthly payments to your savings account. In this case, you would be setting aside $100 each month in anticipation of that $1,200 bill. If it's the type of bill that increases each year, save a little extra each month so you're covered. By making annual payments, you avoid the monthly processing fees, and earn interest on your money in your savings account.

31. Set up payment reminders so you don't miss a payment due date. Paying late will cost you a late payment fee and/or interest on the bill. You can set up reminders in a paper/online calendar, your phone, or by using a special filing system. For my Monthly Bill Payment List, see the Examples section at the back

32. Pay your bills online to save the cost of postage. Remember to initiate this from your own bank account instead of the merchant's website. When you send the funds from your bank, you retain more rights if there's a problem of some kind. If you pay from the merchant's website and there is a problem, you may have trouble fighting this. Once I did this and the amount was incorrect. I was not able to dispute this through my bank because it was a pre-authorized transaction. I learned this lesson the hard way.

33. Have you ever made a credit card purchase with the intention of paying the next statement off in full, but didn't have enough money by the due date? Don't let this happen to you. Make the credit card payment as soon as you have the cash - before you receive your next statement. You can pay a bill anytime, you don't have to wait for the statement. I know people who make a store purchase and go to customer service to pay the bill before they leave the store. It's actually a good tip if you want to avoid the finance charges. We all know that paying finance charges are the enemy of your budget.

34. Enroll in a safe or defensive driving class to lower your auto insurance premium. Contact your auto

insurance company or agent to ask how much it will save you. We have taken the course about every three years to keep our auto insurance affordable. The one we do is about 3 to 4 hours on a Saturday and then we save on our insurance premium for the next three years.

35. Call to inquire when you see changes in billing rates. Our homeowners' insurance bill had increased by over $200. When we called, we were told that the company had raised everyone's rate because of all the weather related claims. We had never placed a claim ourselves, so we asked what we could do to lower the cost. In our case, they recalculated the numbers on the replacement value on the home and found they had calculated too much – the premium was lowered immediately. We asked if there was anything more we could do, and they suggested raising the deductible. We were able to take the rate down another $180 just by making a call and asking questions. One of the best skills you can learn about financial literacy is to advocate for yourself – contact the other party in order to come to a mutually agreeable solution.

36. If you have debt to pay down, consider using cash for all your everyday purchases. You select an amount that you can spend for the week and keep that amount in your wallet in cash. Leave the debit and credit cards at home. If your allowance runs out before the week, then you can't spend anymore. Using cash cuts down your impulse spending and leaves you the money to get your debt paid down quicker. It will make you think twice before making a purchase that may not be necessary.

37. Develop a plan to pay down your debt. First, make a list of all the debts you owe. The list should include creditor, interest rate, balance owed and the minimum payment amount. For a worksheet, see the Examples section at the back. There are two ways to pay down this debt. You can make the highest monthly payment on the debt with the smallest balance. Continue to do this until this debt is paid off. Then, focus on the next smallest balance until you are done. Paying off the small debts quickly will give you the momentum to keep moving forward to payoff your debt. The other way to do this is to focus on the debt or loan with the highest interest rate first. Pay that one off as fast as you can first.

Then go on to the next highest interest rate until all debt is paid off. Paying off the highest interest rate debts first, will save you more money on fees and interest.

Dining Out

38. Do you like eating out? Do you want to pay less? Look for restaurants in your area that allow you to bring your own wine. Alcohol can double your restaurant bill and is the biggest profit for the restaurant. In addition, look for other money saving offers that can save you money on the total bill.

39. Do you feel deprived if you don't eat out? Try eating out for lunch instead of dinner. Lunch menus are almost always less expensive than dinner menus and therefore you will save money and still enjoy eating out.

40. Were you disappointed by a service or product? Tell them about it and they might give you a freebie or a discount on your next purchase. Our local pizza place offered no delivery fee if you ordered online. We needed the order at work within an hour and we were only 3 blocks away and we didn't think it was unreasonable. The delivery took well over an hour. After several polite calls to find the status of the order, we were offered a credit towards a future order. Another time, we purchased food to go (2 sandwiches) and one sandwich was totally wrong and the other had the items we asked to be left off. We contacted the manager and the order was corrected and we received our money back. All it took was a call to express our dissatisfaction with the service. This works on products too. We purchased a portable GPS and the screen died after 16 days. To discuss how disappointed I was with the product and how I relied on this to get to clients. The return policy was 15 days. After expressing my dissatisfaction, the store accepted the return and I was given my money back.

41. Bring food or beverages from home when you know you might be tempted to eat out. When we needed to go upstate for most of the day, we packed some bottled water in a cooler for the ride. This saved us from purchasing marked up bottled water from a machine, gas station or convenience store. We do this for snacks and food too. All it takes is a little more planning and less than 5 minutes to pack.

42. Use coupons or daily deals for dining out. Remember: don't eat out just because you have a coupon. Even with a discount, eating out is more expensive than dining in. Only look for discounts when you have plans to go out or have an upcoming celebration. You can spend more

money just because it's a great deal. So think about how it will work in your budget before making the purchase.

43. Does spending time out with others mean eating out? How about having them come over for dinner instead? You can do anything from drinks and appetizers to a five course meal. You can even have a potluck where everyone brings something so you don't have to do all the cooking. You can also spend time with friends and do something not related to food.

44. We belong to an airline dining program, which means we can earn airline miles by eating out. All we had to do was sign up online and register our credit / debit cards. We choose our restaurant based on which ones are participating that day. No coupons or codes required. Just enjoy your meal, pay with a registered credit card and the miles appear in your account in a few weeks. This is a great way to keep our airline miles account active without flying. It's a great way to dine out in a city you have never been to with the restaurant reviews from other people.

Entertainment

45. What does your community (or region) have to offer? We have free movies at the library every Friday night. In the summer, we have movies in the park where you can bring your own picnic. We can take in a performance at the local theater, go to a parade, and more. We get online newsletters from the Library and Parks & Recreation department that tell us what's happening this month. All with many free opportunities.

46. Will it break the budget to take the family to a professional sporting event? We live in the greater New York area where the price to go to a professional sporting event can be budget breaking for a family. Try going to a minor league or college game instead. The tickets, parking and refreshments are substantially less expensive. For us, a ticket to a baseball game in NY is $125-$200 at field level (that's face value). For the minor league team its $25 for a luxury seat at field level. What a great way to get out and save money.

47. Libraries have kept up with the times. They offer so much more than hardcover and paperback books. Not only can you borrow CDs, DVDs, and videogames, you can also borrow downloadable books for your reader and audio books for your mp3 player. All for free. Check out your local library today. It's the best kept secret in town.

48. Volunteer as an usher at a community theatre and you might see the performance for free. Local community organizations are always looking for volunteers. Take your talents, put them to work, and you may get a benefit for your services. If nothing else, you will meet new people in your community.

49. Check your billing statement envelopes and emails for local coupons. For example, our cable company has "Free Movie Tuesdays" which means we can claim two free tickets to select theaters in the area. Our water company has a newsletter in the monthly bill with discount coupons. We have used 2 for 1 coupons for admission discounts for aquariums and museums. It only takes seconds to scan the contents of the envelope or website for these offers.

Shopping

50. Have you ever noticed that you made a purchase and then you see the item on sale for less? If you purchased something just before it went on sale (typically within a 10-day to 2-week period), you can go back to the store to get credited for the difference. Keep those receipts! Sometimes, stores will even match the competition's pricing. When I purchased my last printer/fax/scanner combo, I price shopped for the best price. Well, that wasn't a store that offered me rewards. So I contacted a store that I was a part of the loyalty program to ask if they price matched. I found out that the same exact item was going on sale the following week.

51. Think off season. Most people shop for summer clothes in the spring and winter clothes in the fall. How about reversing that? You could have your next winter coat at a discount if you buy it in the early spring. This past fall, I was able to buy a pair of shorts for $1.80 and a black cocktail dress for under $5. I was more than happy to find my new clothes in my closet after the long winter. And I certainly have gotten my money's worth out of these items.

52. Shop used versus new. Look at thrift, consignment, and second hand shops for a variety of items. They offer more than clothing. Even better, check out FreeCycle.com or the free section on CraigsList.org. You may be able to get what you want at no cost to you.

53. Negotiate by asking this question when shopping: "Are there any other discounts available for my purchase?" Sometimes, the salesperson or cashier will have a coupon you can use to get an additional discount. We recently went furniture shopping and one particular store was offering an additional 20% off for customers who had a store credit card. I didn't want to sign up for another card, but asked if I could have the discount anyway. They said "yes". An additional 20% off always makes me happy.

54. Do you have any unused gift cards sitting around? Well, use them. Unused gift cards are good business for stores. They have your money and they got to keep their merchandise. If a particular store doesn't offer anything you want, check to see if it's affiliated with other stores. For examples, Home Goods, Marshalls and TJ Maxx

are sister stores - a Marshall's gift card is good at all 3 stores.

55. Sign up for rewards programs. (Consider setting up a separate email account because you will get quite a few promotional messages.) Many stores have frequent shoppers programs. As you walk the aisles in the grocery, pharmacy, hardware stores, etc., you'll see sales prices that may only be available to those in the rewards program. It's worth taking a moment to sign up, but remember you are giving the company your personal information that they will use for marketing purposes.

56. How about repair versus toss? Back in my Grandmother's day, they used to darn clothing to make it last longer. Frankly, I am not a good sewer, but I can sew a button on. I can mend little holes. I just hemmed a pair of curtains. Think about the cost to repair versus the cost to replace, so you might save some money with a tiny bit of work.

57. Make sure you return items that are not what you expected. So many people have clothes in the closet that are too small, too big, or just don't look right because they didn't return them

to get their money back. It's not just clothes. You can return almost anything for a refund or store credit. A while back, when I was moving offices, I found many products that were still in the original package. Unopened, I returned them to my local office supply store for over $100 in store credit to use for future purchases. I learned my lesson after that. What do you have in your home that you don't use?

58.   Senior discounts. Don't be shy, ask. Some airlines offer discounts on airfare, movies have senior pricing, and restaurants have offers for dining. Check out www.AARP.org for more information on senior discounts. This has saved us a great deal of money from hotel reservations to our insurance (car, home and umbrella) and everything in between. We just got a price adjustment for an upcoming vacation because they offered senior pricing ($320 savings). And you don't necessarily have to be 62 or 65.

59.   Are you paying for a membership or subscription that you don't use? Cancel it and save the money. I no longer subscribe to magazines. I rarely have time to read them, but I continued my subscriptions through misplaced feelings of loyalty, guilt, and nostalgia. Now, if I want to

read one of my old favorites, I purchase a copy at the store. That happens maybe two times a year at most. I honestly don't miss them.

Personal Care

60. Use trade schools for personal services. I can get my hair washed and cut by a student at the local cosmetology academy for as much as 75% savings over the local salon. Want a massage? Check the prices at your local massage academy. I know people who go to the college to get dental services and chiropractic treatments from students who are under the supervision of a trained professional.

61. Use free online greeting cards to save the cost of a card and postage. They are easy to send, no need to go to the store or post office, and you can send them day or night. We have used online cards for birthdays, holidays and invites. It's so easy and I can set them up ahead of time so that we don't miss an important date.

62. Walk to do your errands versus driving. We are fortunate to live within a mile of a shopping district. We not only save gas (and car wear and tear) but we get exercise as well. It's a great time to run an errand, walk the dog and get some exercise – all with one simple walk.

Healthcare

63. Think preventative. Regular dental check-ups and cleanings can fend off expensive dental work. Catching a cavity when it's small is more cost effective than having a root canal later.

64. Are you taking a prescription? Shop around for the best pricing. You can look outside the local pharmacy and try grocery stores, warehouse clubs, big box stores, and more. I have personally used www.BidRX.com for some prescriptions. You can find cost effective pricing by shopping pharmacies all over the country. You can ask your doctor for free samples too.

65. Check for Health Fairs in your area. Our hospital has a fair every February where you can get your cholesterol and glucose checked for free. I've seen similar health- check offers at pharmacies and even grocery stores. When healthcare is so expensive, it's nice to have a basic wellness check at a discount or for free.

66. Emergency rooms are the most expensive place to be treated. If your doctor's office isn't open, you may want to consider either Urgent Care facilities or clinics in drug stores. Warning: Use this option only for minor injuries and ailments.

If your life is in immediate danger, please go to the hospital emergency room.

67. Are you trying to lose that last 5 pounds (or maybe more)? Experts say that you should track your food and exercise every day. There are free online trackers like www.MyFitnessPal.com and www.LoseIt.com as well as phone apps (the basic version is free). You will be amazed at what this can do for you.

68. Ask your doctor for samples. If your doctor gives you a prescription to fill at the pharmacy, ask for samples first. How many times have you purchased a prescription only to find that there were side effects or it didn't actually help your condition? Try it before you buy it, and you'll save the expense of buying 2 separate prescriptions for the same ailment.

69. Want to take an exercise class? Check your local library or city Parks and Recreation department. Our Library offers free yoga and tai chi classes (for a small recommended donation). It's a way of trying a class to see if you like that type of exercise.

70. Generic medicine costs less than brand name drugs. Ask your doctor, if your prescription has a

generic version that will work just as the brand name. You may be able to save money.

71. Not feeling well? We make some of our own remedies from ingredients we have in the house. We became believers in home remedies when I had a cough that over-the- counter medicines wouldn't touch. It seemed like nothing helped. I searched online and found a recipe with ingredients from the kitchen. It worked! As with anything, check with your doctor first.

72. Get out and take a walk. Walking is an inexpensive way to exercise. Every town has parks, suburbs, or outlying areas to explore. We love weekends when we can explore a new area and a change of scenery.

73. What does your town offer? We have roller skating on Friday nights and swimming on Saturdays for all residents. If you are 55 or older, the senior center offers free exercise classes like Zumba, water aerobics, yoga, etc. Check with your Parks & Recreation Department, Community Centers and Senior Centers for what your town has to offer. You can check nearby towns as well to see if you can participate.

Pets

74. For our pet medicine, we order medicines online from trusted retailers versus buying at the vet. You can even check out your local warehouse club as mine now carries vet prescriptions at the pharmacy. This works for flea, tick and heartworm medicines too.

75. You can use baking soda instead of dog shampoo. Make a paste with baking soda and water, wet the pet down, rub the mixture into the fur, and then rinse. It's cheaper than pet shampoo. It won't irritate their skin and makes their coat shiny. You'll be amazed at how well it works on mud and odors. We use mineral oil to clean our dog's ears. Check with your vet to see what you can do at home.

Employment

76. Does your company offer product and service discounts? My husband's company offers its employees a discount on their cell phone bill and accessories. All we had to do was present a paystub to get the discount. That is a 17% savings each and every month.

77. Does your company offer an insurance discount? There are discounts on insurance such as homeowners, renters, auto, software, and more. All you have to do is ask your Human Resources department, or read your benefits package. You may be paying more than you need to by not knowing what your company offers.

78. Do you belong to a union? Check to see what benefits they offer. We receive $1,000 towards professional development. For us, that can include conferences, seminars, or even college tuition. Now that I am back at school to finish up my degree, that $1,000 came in handy to pay for the next class.

79. Do you have access to a credit union? They often offer lower interest rates on loans and low to no-cost bank accounts. This could be a substantial savings over the long run.

Education

80. Want to go back to school? Check out your local community college. If you are 62 or older in Connecticut you can take a class for free. I'm not there yet, but I am looking forward to this opportunity in a few years. Our community college offers a Lifetime Learners membership for $40 annually. This includes attending some lectures and use of the gym. That's really helpful to be able to exercise indoors on snowy or rainy days.

81. Thinking about college for yourself or your child? It's never too early to plan for tuition. Start researching scholarships while your child is in High School. Then in their senior year, research financial aid. You can apply for financial aid as early as January if they will be attending college sometime that year. So, start your child's FAFSA in January, and complete it with your income tax information. Every state has its own deadline. (Connecticut's is February 15 for priority consideration). The earlier the better as the money goes quickly.

82. Start at a community college and then transfer to a four year school to complete your degree(s).

With college costs rising, and budgets much tighter, local or in-state community colleges are better for your finances. For example, at our local community college a 3 credit class costs $519 whereas the college I am attending is $1,705. That's a big difference in price.

83. For textbooks, compare costs between new, used or rentals. You can check websites such as Chegg.com, BookRenter.com, eBay.com, and CraigsList.org and more. Use the ISBN number when comparing prices to make sure you have the right edition. (A friend's daughter purchased the wrong edition through an online source.) When the class is over, determine if you want to keep the book, or if you want to resell it. I used the campus bookstore for my first textbook. Imagine my surprise when they weren't interested in buying it back after I was done with it (even though it was being used for the same class the next semester). That was the first and last time I purchased a book at the college book store. Now, I compare website pricing and rental periods to find the best deal for me. You can do this too.

84. Do you want to go back to college but can't afford it? See if you qualify for an Individual.

Development Account (IDA). These accounts help low-to-moderate income individuals and families save for specific asset-building purposes. One of those assets is for post-secondary / higher education. If you've met all the qualifications and met your savings goals, you'll receive matching funds from the program. That's free money towards your education.

Income

85. Got stuff that you are not using? Sell those items online for extra cash. We have sold everything from toothbrush heads to a car online. I am always amazed at what other people will buy, and how far they will travel. We sold our plastic container set to someone in Minnesota, tooth brush replacement heads to someone from Manhattan, and much much more.

86. Hold a tag / yard sale. Ask your neighbors to join you and you can have a block sale to really draw in the crowds. If you don't have a lot to sell, consider a "community sale" if there's one in your location. Our town has a community sale every year in the parking lot at the beach where you can pay for a space to sell your items. The event draws many more than I would get in my driveway.

87. Check for unclaimed money. Money in an account that is untouched for 3 years has to be turned over to the state. To find unclaimed money, check www.Unclaimed. org. I found money on unclaimed.org twice. First, stocks I inherited were turned over to unclaimed money. Then, after my father passed away, we found one of his old life insurance policies. Remember: there is never a fee to collect funds.

88. Check for unclaimed pensions. My father retired from the U.S. Postal Service and he received a pension until he passed away. That was easy for us to find. But there are other seniors who receive more than one pension because they changed companies over the years. Do you remember if you signed up for a pension at your first job? Do you know all the places your parents have worked? See if you or anyone in your family has an unclaimed pension at www.pbgc.gov.

89. Thinking of starting a side business? Consider something you are good at, that you enjoy doing, and that you can run from home. For example, I know people who offer baking and graphic design work from home for additional income. Some people rent themselves out for spring or fall gardening, or handyman jobs. If you want to try running a side business, make it something that doesn't require a lot of startup cash to begin.

Savings / Retirement

90. Are you passing up free money? If your employer offers matching funds for your retirement plan, make sure you take advantage of it. I recently made my employment official after working as a consultant for a few years. Now, I am a part time employee and have all the benefits of working for a company. I have a matching retirement plan. I contribute 5% pre-tax money and the company contributes 8% matching funds. That's something I couldn't pass up. You should always do what is needed to get the free matching money that your company offers.

91. Have you been promising yourself that you'll boost your savings, but find there's nothing left at the end of month to save? You are not alone. Automate your savings. Have your employer direct deposit your paycheck into two accounts: checking and savings. If your employer cannot split your paycheck into two accounts, no problem! You can have your bank do it. Set up an automatic transfer from checking to savings every payday. As David Bach, the Author of "The Automatic Millionaire" will tell you: "Pay yourself first." This works for us, and it will for you too.

92. Keep your savings account far from your checking account. Don't keep your savings in the same bank as your checking account. Keep it across town in an area that isn't on your way. It will help if they require a 24 hour wait on online transfers. Making it difficult to access may mean you will think twice about spending it on a "want".

93. Another savings tactic is to not link your savings account to your ATM card. If you have to wait, or make a physical effort to withdraw money, it will make you think twice before you spend.

94. Are you over 50 years old? If so, you can increase your pre-tax contributions to your retirement and health savings accounts (H-S-A) to get them caught up to where you'd like them to be. Amounts change annually, so check online or with your tax preparer for the current year's limits.

95. Do you qualify for an Individual Development Account (IDA)? IDAs are savings accounts that are available to low-to-moderate income families to help them save for a specific purpose. They can be used to save for higher education, a down payment on a home, or to start a business. As

you save, your money is matched, which doubles your savings and helps you get ahead faster. Check out your state's requirements to see if you qualify.

Banking & Credit

96. You can monitor your credit for free. Order your credit report 3 times a year and review it yourself. If you keep forgetting to do it, sign up for my bi-weekly newsletter and you'll receive a reminder email to order your credit report that will help you to stay on top of your credit. **www.JillRussoFoster.com**

97. Do you frequent an ATM machine? Using another bank's ATM can cost you a fee. Save the fees and only use your bank's ATM. This may take some planning, but it will be cost effective to your budget.

98. You're nowhere near your bank's ATMs, but you need cash. Some stores will allow you to get cash back with a purchase if you use your debit card (without charging you a fee). Just make sure you buy something you actually need so you aren't wasting money.

99. Curious about your credit score? If you want a free close approximation of your score, try www.CreditKarma.com, www.Quizzle.com or www.CreditSesame.com. You won't receive your actual FICO score, but it will be close enough to satisfy your curiosity. There's no need to pay a

fee for it. Be careful and don't sign up for any services that will cost you money.

100. Did you know that the higher your credit score, the less you pay overall? Sure, it affects your rates on a loan, but a high score may give you an edge on a good apartment or a good job. Landlords and some employers look at credit scores to see if you are a financially responsible person. Your score will also affect your insurance rates, and that includes home, renters, auto, etc. and many other areas that you wouldn't think of. Bottom line: a higher score means more money in your pocket.

101. Are you paying bank maintenance fees? If the answer is "yes", then it's time to change banks. Shop around to find a bank or credit union with free checking and savings. You may even find a bank that gives you interest on your checking account. There is no need to pay the bank a maintenance fee or any other fees with your account.

Travel

102. Want to earn airline miles even when you're not flying? Many airlines have a website where you can link to your favorite stores and earn miles while shopping online. I have personally earned thousands of miles this way. As an added bonus, I'm keeping my frequent flyer account active between flights, so my miles won't expire when I'm not traveling. A few years back we took a trips to Hawaii and Europe- long expensive flight from the east coast using miles. Thanks to the online shopping option, we had enough miles to fly first class for free.

103. Use your miles and points to travel. I have to admit that it can be overwhelming to coordinate miles and points for the whole trip, but it is well worth it. We went to Europe last summer using airline miles to fly business class, and hotel points to stay at nice hotels before and after our cruise. For the cruise itself, we traded in our timeshare points. We had a great vacation, and we only paid purchase taxes! What's not to like about that?

104. Are you visiting a new city? Try the free walking tours instead of going on a paid tour. We have done this in several European cities and Bermuda too. The tour guides were great, we had time to stop and gawk, and we felt we had experienced the cities in a personal way. You'll meet the locals and learn so much by doing this.

105. Packing for a trip by air has become a challenge. You want to bring everything you need, but you don't want to pay the checked baggage fee. I've learned to pare things down. For example, when planning clothing, I pick three colors so that all items can be mixed and matched. That way I have more outfits with fewer clothes. For a copy of My Travel Packing List, see the Examples section at the back

106. Want to visit a National Park? They have Free Entrance Days a few times a year. To plan your visit, go to www.nps.gov for information on travel, lodging and park events. There are quite a few parks I have to visit before I finish my bucket list.

107. Traveling by car? There are three things you can do to save money at the pump. First, go online to www.GasBuddy.com to check local prices.

Second, use cash because some gas stations charge more for debit / credit card purchases. Finally, pump your own gas. In Connecticut, the difference can be 10¢ per gallon for full service. It all adds up and you want to save as much as you can.

108. If you are like me, you purchase non-refundable airfare. Does that mean you'll be stuck paying the full amount if the price goes down after you buy your tickets? Not necessarily, typically, you can get either a refund or voucher for the difference, after you pay the change fee. To track airline prices, try www.Yapta.com

109. The same is true for cruises. We have an upcoming cruise. Since buying our tickets, I have received 3 decreases in price. I'm not aware of any website that will track cruise ticket prices for you - I just check periodically. The cruise is paid in installments, so there's no need to receive a refund. We simply owe less and less as the price drops. If the price lowers again after the final payment is made, we'll receive the difference in credit to use on board. On this particular cruise, we have a $320 on-board credit. Our cruise line has told us that the prices can change as often as 4 times per day, so don't overwhelm yourself.

Just check in periodically to possibly save yourself some money.

110. Did you recently change your name? If you purchased your passport within a year of your name change, you can get an updated passport for free. This works really well for people who recently got married or divorced.

111. Are you staying in a hotel or rental with a kitchen? When we do, we bring a few essential kitchen supplies to make the most of the convenience. I am talking about non-perishables like paper goods and spices. We bring ketchup, mustard and mayo, but it's in one-time use packets which don't need to be refrigerated and are easy (and safe) to pack. Single serving options are always best for travel - even if you put them together yourself to save money. For salt, pepper and spices, I use a daily pill holder and label each compartment with the spice name so that premium suitcase space isn't wasted on bottles. For paper goods, we pack only what we need - we don't bring a 100 pack of paper plates if we only need 20. For a copy of Time sharing Packing List, see the Examples section at the back.

Bonus

Budgeting

▪ **Track your spending.** I know you are thinking, "I don't have time for that." I can't stress this enough: you need to make the time. You can track your spending in a number of ways. Keep a notebook with you. Use the envelope method (get receipts for all purchases and put them in an envelope). Use a smart phone app. The choice is yours. Now take all those expenses and compile into a budget to know where your money is going. You will find that tracking makes you think twice before spending money. For a copy of my budget sheet, see the Examples section at the back.

▪ **Determine if you have a surplus or shortfall in your monthly budget.** Do you have money left over, or are you pulling from your emergency savings or credit cards just to get by? Are some months different than others? Use my budget tracker to see where you stand.

For a copy of my budget sheet, see the Examples section at the back

■ **Use cash.** Earlier, I suggested using cash at the grocery store. Try using it for all your shopping and entertainment. You set an amount for a specific time period (a pay period, a month, etc.) and give yourself that amount in cash. If the money runs out, you can't spend until the next period. It really makes you think about how you spend your money, and it's the easiest way to make your income stretch to meet your needs.

■ **Institute a "Don't Buy Anything" week.** It will help you find the leaks in your budget. Make it a game to see who in the household can go the longest without spending money. (Continue to pay for your legitimate expenses like your mortgage / rent, utilities etc.) Judith Levine wrote a book called *"Not Buying It: My Year Without Spending"*. Read the book for some real eye-opening inspiration. One great book that I read years back was *"The Complete Tightwad Gazette"* by Amy Dacyczyn. It's a compilation of her newsletters promoting frugal living. While I don't think of myself as "frugal", I have used many of her tips successfully in my own household.

Taxes

 Do you have a simple tax return? If you do, you should look for a VITA tax preparer (Volunteer Income Tax Assistance) in your community. Check them out to see if you meet their guidelines. If so, you could have your taxes done for free.

 If you make donations (cash or items), please keep good records so you can claim them as a tax deduction. For cash donations, a cancelled check, bank or credit card statement usually is sufficient. For items, make a list, take photos, and then determine the value of the item(s) you are donating. Non-profit organizations can help by giving you a letter or receipt for your donation. Your tax preparer will be able to tell you what type of documentation is needed for each type of donation.

 We would love to hear from you. Tell us what you do personally to save money. You can contact us at Book@JillRussoFoster.com.

Examples

Bill Checklist

Date Rec'd	Date Paid	Accounts	Date Due	Amount	How Paid	Acct User Name/Password

My Weekly Meal Planner

	Sun	Mon	Tues	Wed	Thurs	Fri	Sat
Breakfast							
Lunch							
Snack							
Dinner							

ITEMS TO BUY

Travel Packing List

CLOTHING / ACCESSORIES

x	Item	Notes
	Underwear / Bras	
	Socks / Pantyhose	
	Pajamas / Robe	
	Swimsuits / Cover up / Beach Bag	
	Gym / Workout gear	
	Raincoat / Coat / Gloves / Scarf / Hat	
	Sweater / Jacket	
	Business Outfit(s)	
	Evening Outfit(s)	
	Casual Outfit(s)	
	Shoes	

MONEY & DOCUMENTS

x	Item	Notes
	Airline Tickets / Hotel Confirmations	
	Discount Coupons / Reward Cards / AA Dining	
	Itinerary / Tour Confirmations / Receipt Envelope	
	Driver's License / Passport	
	Maps / GPS	

Jill Russo Foster

TOILETRIES

x	Item	Notes
	Teeth: Toothbrush / Paste / Floss	
	Hair: Shampoo / Conditioner / Brush	
	Skin: Face Care / Moisturizer / Suntan Lotion	
	Shower: Razor / Cream / Deodorant	
	Make-up / Jewelry	
	First Aid: Aspirin / Band-Aids / Bug Repellant	

LAST MINUTE ITEMS / ELECTRONICS

x	Item	Notes
	Fruit / Snacks / Water Bottles	
	Cell Phones / Charger	
	Prescription Medication	
	Book / Reading Material	
	Sunglasses / Eyeglasses	
	Camera / Charger / Memory Sticks / Cables	
	Movies / Adapter / iPod	
	Binoculars / Ear Phones for Plane	
	Laptop / Tablet / Charger	
	Airplane – Blanket / Pillow	
	Towel Chair Clips	

Time Share Packing List

Meal Planning Chart

Day	Breakfast	Lunch	Dinner	Snacks
Day 1				
Day 2				
Day 3				
Day 4				
Day 5				
Day 6				
Day 7				

Shopping & Packing List (Food)

x	Item	Additional items
	Salt & Pepper	
	Protein Powder	
	Spices	
	Coffee / Tea	
	Sugar	
	Snacks	
	Ketchup / Mustard / Mayo	
	Soda	
	Water	
	Juice	
	Milk	
	Eggs	
	Meat	
	Salad Stuff	
	Dressing	

Bread	
Vegetables	

Shopping & Packing List (Incidentals)

x	Item	Where is it packed?
	Paper Plates	
	Napkins	
	Plastic Silverware	
	Aluminum Foil	
	Plastic Bags	
	Plastic Containers	
	Water Bottles	
	Cleaning Products	
	Chip Clips	
	Towel Chair Clips	
	Grocery Bags	
	Rafts / Noodles / Water Toys	

Notes

Travel Planning To-Do List

Planning the Trip

x	Item	Notes
	Make reservations – flight / seat, cruise, hotel, car, tours, airport parking or transportation to the airport, entertainment / dinner reservations etc.	
	Passport – make sure it's current, you typically can't travel on a passport with less than 6 month to the expiration date	
	Determine if you want to purchase trip insurance	
	Contact your car insurance and/or credit card company to see if you are covered for your rental car (if you are, you may want to decline some rental car insurance coverage from the rental car company	

Home Arrangements

x	Item	Notes
	House sitter or someone to check in on your home	
	Pet and plant care in your absence	
	Postal Mail and Newspaper holds	
	Let your local Police Dept. that you will be out of town	
	Lock windows and doors	
	Shut off or unplug electronics that will not be in use	
	Adjust thermostat and water heater	

Documentation

x	Item	Notes
	Airline tickets and boarding passes – save time by checking in online ahead of time and reserve your seat if you haven't done so already	
	Passport / Visas with copies kept separately with you and another set left with someone you trust	
	Consent if you are traveling out of the country with a family or friend's minor child (you will need this too if you are divorced)	
	Driver's License	
	Hotel / Timeshare Confirmation	
	Car Rental Confirmation	
	Wallet –remove what you don't need with you. For what you are taking, make copies with phone numbers and leave with someone you trust. Make sure you bring a copy with you that you keep separate in case you need to cancel them if they are lost or stolen	
	Medical Information – insurance cards for medical	
	Prescriptions – make sure they are in their original bottles for Customs	
	Eyeglasses	
	Credit Cards – contact them to let them know the details of your trip so that they will not decline your transactions	
	Register with the State Department if you are traveling out of the country	

Luggage

x	Item	Notes
	Make sure all luggage has identification tags on the outside and inside too. Remember to do this with carry on and other cases (briefcases, camera etc.). This should include your name, home address, home/ cell phone and include the information for where you are staying that that phone.	
	Weigh your luggage before you leave the house. Airlines charge fees for overweight luggage and that can be costly. Make sure you are under the limit – you may want to wear the heavier clothing.	

Money

x	Item	Notes
	Cash –have small bills for small purchases and tipping	
	Credit Cards / Debit Cards / ATM – Let them know where you are traveling so that your transactions will be approved	
	Travelers Checks	
	Foreign Currency for the countries you be visiting. Even if there is better exchange rate at your destination, you should have some cash with you when you enter the country.	
	Plastic bag for wet clothing	
	Water proof case for valuables	
	Sewing kits for quick repairs	
	First aid kit to include items for minor injuries (cuts, scraps, bug bites, blisters etc.)	

Clothing

x	Item	Notes
	Under garments – underwear, bras, t-shirts, sock, pantyhose etc.	
	Shoes / sandals / slippers / walking / beach	
	Pants / jeans	
	Shirts	
	Sweater / jacket / rain gear	
	Dress Up – suit / dress	
	Swimwear – swimsuit / cover up / beach bag / hat / lotion	
	Sleepwear	
	Sports clothes	

Toiletries

x	Item	Notes
	Teeth – toothbrush / toothpaste / floss.	
	Hair – shampoo / conditioner / brush / comb / dryer / styling products / clips	
	Body – deodorant / moisturizer	
	Face – cleanser / lotion / make up / perfume	
	Bug repellant	
	First aid products – band aids / antibacterial creams	

Debt Repayment Plan

Name of Card / Loan	Balance Owed	Interest Rate	Payment Amount	Months to Pay Off	Years to Pay Off
VISA	$5,000.00	12.0%	-$100.00	69.7	5 Years, 10 Months
Car Loan	$20,000.00	4.0%	-$300.00	75.5	6 Years, 4 Months
MasterCard	$25,000.00	16.0%	-$400.00	135.3	11 Years, 4 Months

Monthly Budget Planner

Directions: Choose a time period (e.g. yearly or monthly). Type in your regular income and expenses. *Remember to use the same time period for income and expenses.*

INCOME		Home Expenses		Auto Expenses		Insurance Expenses	
Pay (Take Home)	$	Mortgage	$	Car Payment #1	$	Home	$
Commission	$	Home Equity	$	Car Payment #2	$	Renters	$
Bonuses	$	Property Taxes	$	Gas	$	Mortgage	$
Alimony	$	Rent	$	Maint. / Repairs	$	Life	$
Child Support	$	Condo Fees	$	Parking	$	Health	$
Unemployment	$	Phone	$	Tolls / EZ Pass	$	Disability	$
Social Security	$	Fax	$	Emergency Rd Serv.	$	Long Term Care	$
Pension	$	Cell	$	Radio	$	Dental	$
Dividends	$	Internet	$	Tickets	$	Vision	$
Interest	$	Cable	$	Driver's License	$	Prescriptions	$
Rental Income	$	Electricity	$	Car Registration	$	Auto	$
	$	Water	$		$	Boat / RV	$
	$	Gas	$		$	Pet	$
Total Income	**$ 0.00**	Heat	$	**Total Auto**	**$ 0.00**		$
		Trash	$				$
Debt/Loans		Repairs	$	**Health Expenses**		**Total Insurance**	**$ 0.00**
Credit Card #1	$	Snow Removal	$	Gym Membership	$	**Personal Care Expenses**	
Credit Card #2	$	Landscaping	$	Dentist	$	Haircuts / Salon	$
Credit Card #3	$	Alarm	$	Doctor	$	Cosmetics	$
401K Loan	$	Pool / Hot Tub	$	Medications	$	Hygiene	$
Student Loan #1	$		$	Home Health Care	$	Personal Care	$
Student Loan #2	$		$	Nurse	$	Massages	$
	$		$	Medical Equipment	$	Manicures	$
	$		$		$		$
Total Debt/Loans	**$ 0.00**	**Total Home**	**$ 0.00**	**Total Health**	**$ 0.00**	**Total Pers. Care**	**$ 0.00**

Remember to use the same time period for each expense.

Child Expenses

School / Tuition	$
Room / Board	$
Books / Supplies	$
Lunch	$
School Uniforms	$
Sports Fees	$
Sports Equipment	$
Extracurricular	$
	$
	$
Total Child	**$ 0.00**

Clothing Expenses

Clothes	$
Shoes	$
Accessories	$
Jewelry	$
	$
	$
Total Clothing	**$ 0.00**

Savings Account Deposits

Emergency Fund	$
Education	$
Auto Purchase	$
Home Purchase	$
Vacation	$
Retirement	$
	$
	$
Total Savings Dep.	**$ 0.00**

Food Expenses

Groceries	$
Fast Food	$
Restaurant	$
Take Out	$
Alcohol	$
	$
Total Food	**$ 0.00**

Other Expenses

Birthdays	$
Weddings	$
Anniversaries	$
Gifts	$
Decorations	$
Donations	$
Gambling / Lottery	$
Postage	$
	$
	$
	$
	$
Total Other	**$ 0.00**

Entertainment Expenses

Books / Magazines	$
Newspapers	$
Movie Rental	$
Video Games	$
Computer	$
Software	$
Events / Tickets	$
Movies	$
Music	$
	$
	$
Total Entertainmen	**$ 0.00**

Pet Expenses

Food	$
Veterinarian	$
Toys	$
Treats	$
License	$
	$
	$
Total Pet	**$ 0.00**

Total Income $	0.00
MINUS	-
Total Expenses $	0.00
EQUALS	=
Net Results $	0.00

Yearly Budget Planner

Directions: As you track each month, write the totals here. The Year to Date totals will automatically appear.

	JAN	FEB	MAR	APR	MAY	JUN	JUL	AUG	SEP	OCT	NOV	DEC
INCOME	$											
Debt/Loans	$											
Home	$											
Auto	$											
Health	$											
Insurance	$											
Personal Care	$											
Child	$											
Entertainment	$											
Clothing	$											
Food	$											
Pet	$											
Savings Account	$											
Other	$											
Monthly Totals	$ 0.00	0.00	0.00	0.00	0.00	0.00	0.00	0.00	0.00	0.00	0.00	0.00
Year to Date	$ 0.00	0.00	0.00	0.00	0.00	0.00	0.00	0.00	0.00	0.00	0.00	0.00

Notes:

www.ingramcontent.com/pod-product-compliance
Lightning Source LLC
Chambersburg PA
CBHW021003180526
45163CB00005B/1870